PowerHiking

SAN FRANCISCO

*TWELVE GREAT WALKS
THROUGH THE STREETS OF
SAN FRANCISCO
AND ENVIRONS*

CAROLYN HANSEN **CATHLEEN PECK**

PowerHiking
SAN FRANCISCO
is dedicated to
John and Rodney

Art direction and design	**Dennis Gallagher and John Sullivan**
	Visual Strategies, San Francisco
Maps	**Kina Sullivan**
Photography	**Carolyn Hansen**
Copy Editor	**George Marsh**
Additional photos	**photo stock**
Printer	**NORCAL Printing, San Francisco**
	Printed in China
Publisher	**PowerHiking Ltd.**

PowerHiking

FOREWORD

This book was created for all visitors to San Francisco, including those who live in and around the City. Even though we have lived in the San Francisco Bay Area for many years, we saw San Francisco with new eyes while writing this book. The research that we did was fascinating and exciting for us. The City keeps evolving and there are always interesting places to visit, such as AT+T Park and the South of Market area, and the de Young Museum in Golden Gate Park. However, the main reason that we saw and learned new things was that we were *PowerHiking,* and not just driving through to a destination. On foot, and with the desire to learn about culture, history, and to imagine life in San Francisco in days gone by, we had such a good time. We hope that you will too!

On our **PowerHikes** we used a GPS device to keep track of time and distance, a street map for marking the way, and diligently noted the names of shops and restaurants. There may be slight variations as you do the hikes and slight differences in your destinations. Everyone walks at a different pace and will spend more or less time exploring certain areas of interest. The names of stores, cafés, and restaurants may change somewhat. For the most part, San Francisco remains the same. Any mistakes in the directions or the maps are ours, and we hope you will forgive small inaccuracies.

We are again thankful to our Power Partners, John and Rodney, who have been so supportive of our endeavors. We appreciate the excellent work and creativity of our production team, John Sullivan and Dennis Gallagher.

There are so many excellent books that cover special aspects of San Francisco, and we wish to acknowledge some that were helpful to us. They are *Stairway Walks in San Francisco* by Adah Bakalinsky; *Walking San Francisco on the Barbary Coast Trail* by Daniel Bacon; *Historic Walks in San Francisco* by Rand Richards; *Walking San Francisco* by Liz Gans and Rick Newby; and *Walking San Francisco* by Tom Downs. We highly recommend them for a more in-depth understanding of this beautiful City.

Carolyn Hansen, Cathleen Peck

THINGS TO KNOW, BEFORE YOU GO

WEATHER AND YOUR "LOOK"

Although San Francisco is in sunny California, it is a Northern California city and its summer weather is usually not the balmy weather associated with Southern California. The proximity of the City to the Pacific Ocean, the prevailing winds, and the warmer inland valleys produce in the summer months what is affectionately known as "natural air conditioning" or *fog*. Mark Twain is credited with saying, "The coldest winter I ever experienced was summer in San Francisco." Here is how to be prepared.

• It is best not to wear shorts in the City of San Francisco. While appropriate in the warmer suburbs, they are generally not warm enough. Longer pants and walking shoes will make you more comfortable. There are warm days but, in summer, be prepared for fog and cool breezes.

• Dress in layers. Do not be fooled by the California sun as weather conditions can change suddenly. The fog is cool but usually burns off and the days are pleasant until the fog rolls in again. Wear a sweater or jacket for mornings, and shed them for the afternoons. You will need a jacket again in the evenings. In contrast to summer, the spring and fall can be quite pleasant and warm. Winter is chilly and rainy. If you go out on the Bay, it is always chilly. Be prepared. The sun and wind can fool you, and remember the sunscreen.

CAREFUL

Like all large urban centers, there are some neighborhoods that are not visitor-friendly. *POWERHIKING SAN FRANCISCO* does not lead you into these neighborhoods. However, good advice for any City is to always be aware of your surroundings, keep close guard of your valuables, and ignore those asking for money. The City provides a full spectrum of services for the poor and homeless. If in doubt, check with the concierge at the hotel.

NOTE: If you want to fit in, do not say FRISCO, or SAN FRAN.

TRANSPORTATION
The City has a bus and trolley service, MUNI (San Francisco Municipal Railway), which provides bus, trolley, and cable car service. It will take you around downtown and to most tourist and shoreline destinations. The cable cars are great fun and there are several lines to choose from. Have cash on hand for the fare. The old-time trolley cars run along The Embarcadero and Market Street and are practical and fun. BART (Bay Area Rapid Transit) is also available in the City, to the South Bay, to the East Bay, to San Francisco International Airport, and to Oakland International Airport.

Schedules and destinations can be found on the website. There are also numerous ferries that ply the Bay and you can spend memorable days and evenings on water excursions. Fun vehicles for getting around, and available for rental in the Fisherman's Wharf area, are the Electric Time Car (two or four seats) and the GOCAR (two seats and three wheels with GPS and storytelling). There are also numerous locations for bicycle rentals. San Francisco CityPASS is a worthwhile investment.

FOOD
San Francisco is known for good food and excellent restaurants. Try to sample the varieties that it offers. Many restaurants specialize in locally grown, organic produce and meats, and there is delicious seafood. Try to make every meal special!

WHAT IS POWERHIKING?

PowerHiking is choosing to walk with a big agenda. It takes sightseeing to a new level of energy and interest. It is walking with a purpose that excites not only your senses but also your spirit as you visit a special neighborhood, a beautiful park, or an iconic destination, such as the Golden Gate Bridge! When you *PowerHike* in San Francisco, you are going to have an exciting, exhilarating experience. Some walks take you to architectural wonders, such as the Transamerica Pyramid building, or the de Young Museum. Others take you into the beautifully preserved natural landscape surrounding the City. Still others explore the many diverse cultures that contribute so much to the vitality and flavors of the City. Along the way, fascinating history is all around you, whether it is the old buildings from the Barbary Coast, the Victorian homes in Pacific Heights, or the ruins of the Sutro Baths at Lands End.

You may choose to spend only a few hours exploring the City, or follow the longer routes that take you through many famous sites, such as the *PowerHike* along the Bay from Fort Mason through Aquatic Park and Fisherman's Wharf, continuing along The Embarcadero and up Telegraph Hill to Coit Tower. There is so much history, tantalizing food, and extraordinary sights, the walks are unforgettable.

Aside from the thoroughly enjoyable places you go, the best part of *PowerHiking* is how good it feels to be walking and moving at your own pace, stopping when you want to stop and look, eat, shop, or take photos. You are in charge of your experience! It does not mean that you will not take a bus, cable car or taxi to get started or after a long day, but the walk itself is its own reward and you will delight in your exhilaration and sense of accomplishment. So put on your *PowerHiking* shoes, take a bottle of water, a camera, this book, and head out for your first *PowerHike* in San Francisco!

CONTENTS

PowerHiking | SAN FRANCISCO

CHAPTER 1

THE GOLDEN GATE BRIDGE

| DISTANCE **9.5** MILES | TIME **6** HOURS |

THE PALACE OF FINE ARTS

CRISSY FIELD

GOLDEN GATE PROMENADE

FORT POINT

THE GOLDEN GATE BRIDGE

* This walk is a long PowerHike and

can be separated into two —

Crissy Field and the Bridge itself.

This *PowerHike* is bursting with beauty. From the very first step there is one spectacular view after another. Start at The Palace of Fine Arts. On land belonging to the Presidio of San Francisco, this beautiful rotunda was built for the Pan Pacific International Exposition in 1915, celebrating the completion of the Panama Canal and the rebuilding of the City of San Francisco following the devastation of the 1906 earthquake and fire. The Beaux Arts structure was designed by famous San Francisco architect Bernard

Maybeck. Wander to the left around the reflecting lake and follow the

path through the park. There are many ducks, birds and local people enjoying the beauty of this idyllic setting, now an iconic part of the San Francisco skyline. After circling the rotunda pass the **Exploratorium**, a world-renowned science and learning museum, relocating to Pier 15 in spring 2013. Cross Marina Boulevard at Lyon Street and walk through the park, passing the St. Francis Yacht Club, admiring the beauty of the yacht harbor and the exhilarating locale

of the club. Turn left and begin the

Bay trail known as the Golden Gate

Promenade. With the Bay on your

right and the Presidio on your left,

this is an incredibly spectacular

walk. As you cross the footbridge you will see the tidal marsh on the left,

home to many species of birds. Beyond the tidal

marsh is a large grass expanse known as **Crissy Field**. Built in 1919, Crissy Field has seen the landing of the first flight around the world, and the take-off of the first flight to Hawaii. Stunts, air races, and test planes are also a part of the history of Crissy Field. Crowds flocked to the grass field by the Bay to watch the beginnings of the aviation industry. On the left are hangars, barracks and public sports facilities such as a climbing wall and trampoline. On the right you will see the **National Marine Sanctuary** and Gulf of the Farallones Visitor Center, open Wednesday through Sunday 10 a.m. to 4 p.m. Go inside, as the information on marine and bird life in the Bay and the Farrallon Islands is fascinating. Also on the water side, is the old Coast Guard station and, just beyond, the fishing pier. Walking out on the pier you feel like you are standing in the middle of the Bay, with incredible views of water, the City, Marin County, and the Golden Gate Bridge. To the left of the trail is the popular Warming Hut, a friendly place for a snack, and a nature-oriented shop.

The trail becomes Marine Drive which leads along the sea wall to Fort Point. This is the spot where Kim Novak jumped into the

water in Alfred Hitchcock's famous film, *Vertigo*. Fort Point is located at the base of the south tower of the Golden Gate Bridge and it is quite amazing to look up at the massive structure and hear the roar of the cars above. The only fort on the West Coast, Fort Point was built in 1853 to protect the Bay from Confederate attack during the Civil War.

Though outfitted with over one hundred cannon, and with brick walls several feet thick, it never saw battle. Used for training, storage, and to guard mine fields and the

Golden Gate anti-submarine net during

World War II, Fort Point today is a

monument to another era. Tours are

given by the Park Rangers, and there is

fascinating instruction on how to load

and fire the cannon. On the main level

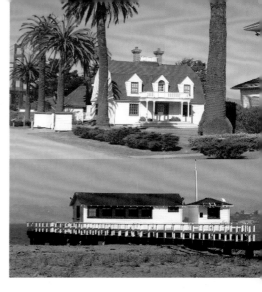

is a wonderful bookstore filled with historical information on the fort,

and on the second and third levels are examples of officer and enlisted

man quarters, and an exhibit of photographs depicting the history of

the infantry at the fort, the Buffalo Soldiers, and the role of women in

the Army. Continue up the stairs to the top of the fort. The views are

breathtaking and well-worth the effort. Not only do you have an incredible look at the underside of the Golden Gate Bridge, but also views of the Bay in every direction.

Begin your *PowerHike* across one of the most recognizable structures

in the world and symbol of San Francisco. As you leave Fort Point, it is a natural point to choose to continue the *PowerHike* to the Golden Gate Bridge or return on the Promenade to the Palace of Fine Arts. A walk across the Golden Gate Bridge can be a day's activity in itself and this chapter can be divided into two separate walks. Crossing the Bridge adds 5 miles to the

4 1/2 you have already walked. To continue

on the exhilarating walk across the Bridge,

walk .4 of a mile along the Bay back from Fort

Point towards Crissy Field. On the left is the

Warming Hut, perfect for a snack and some

browsing through the nature-oriented shop.

Across the street and uphill from the Warming

Hut is a sign directing you up to the East Battery and the Golden Gate

Bridge Walkway. Follow the signage as it is quite good. The Bridge is not

a difficult walk and well worth the effort as the views are magnificent.

It is .4 miles from the bottom of the stairs to the Golden Gate Bridge

Plaza, which leads to the pedestrian walkway across the Bridge. At the Plaza is a fascinating historical exhibit on Bridge construction, the **Bridge Pavillion** (visitor center and shop), the **Bridge Café**, and, just above by the start of the Bridge Walkway, the Round House, home to a

virtual bridge experience. It is 1.7 miles to Vista Point in Marin County on the north end of the bridge and the walkway is open only during daylight hours. The views in all directions are spectacular, particularly up to the top of the towers. If you are lucky, there will be no fog swirling around

and you might see a tanker or cargo

ship heading under the bridge

and out to sea. One of the most

astounding feats of engineering of

its time, the Golden Gate Bridge

was completed in 1937. Joseph Strauss was

the chief engineer and there is a statue of

him in the plaza. You will see workmen on

the bridge as maintenance is constant and painting

is a full-time job. Return to the Warming Hut, Crissy

Field, and the Palace of Fine Arts, the end of an

exciting *PowerHike*.

CHAPTER 2

FISHERMAN'S WHARF

DISTANCE 6 MILES | **TIME 6 HOURS**

AQUATIC PARK

FORT MASON

HYDE STREET PIER

GHIRARDELLI SQUARE

THE CANNERY

FISHERMAN'S WHARF

PIER 39

THE EMBARCADERO

TELEGRAPH HILL

COIT TOWER

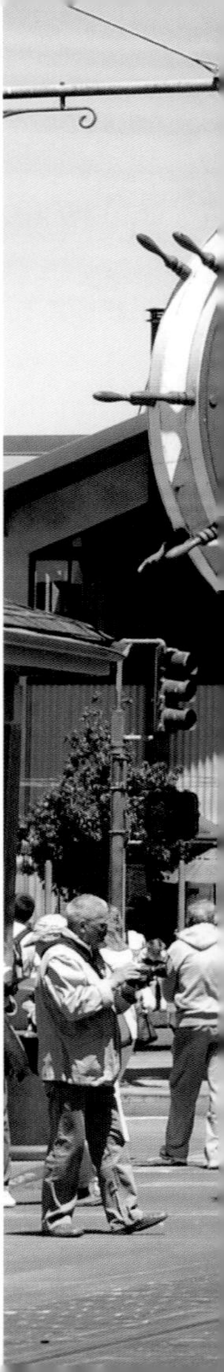

San Francisco Bay

Pier 39

Municipal Pier

Hyde Street Pier

Fisherman's Wharf

Fort Mason & Golden Gate National Recreational Area

Aquatic Park

Jefferson St

Beach St

N Point St

The Embarcadero

Ghirardelli Square

The Cannery

Van Ness Ave

Francisco St

Chestnut St

Larkin St

Polk St

Hyde St

Leavenworth St

Jones St

Taylor St

Mason St

Powell St

Columbus Ave

Stockton St

Grant Ave

Kearny St

Montgomery St

Greenwich St

Coit Tower

Filbert St

Union St

Lombard St

Greenwich St

Filbert St

Union St

Green St

Vallejo St

Broadway

Jackson St

Washington St

Gough St

Franklin St

Van Ness Ave

Polk St

Larkin St

Hyde St

Pacific Ave

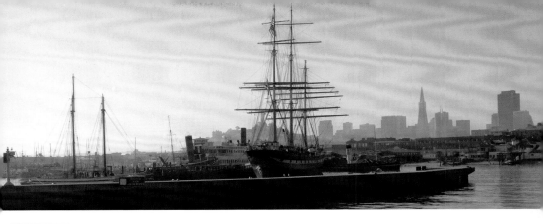

This *PowerHike* explores a variety of San Francisco neighborhoods. You navigate the diversity of a former bayside Army post, the tourist mecca of Ghirardelli Square and Fisherman's Wharf, and the eclectic residential neighborhood of Telegraph Hill and Coit Tower. It is relatively gentle terrain, with just one daunting stairway leading up to Coit Tower. Worth the effort, Coit Tower views are fabulous and the staircase down is magical! Start at the Hyde Street cable car turn-around near the Hyde Street Pier.

In front of you is **Aquatic Park**, officially known as the San Francisco

Maritime National Historic Park. Aquatic Park was built in 1939 and is

set in a picturesque cove, the beach of which is enjoyed year round by

swimmers, members of the decades old Dolphin Swimming and Rowing

Club. *PowerHike* to the left along the promenade. The Aquatic Park

Boathouse building is on the right. Completed in 1939, it is a beautiful

art deco structure built to look like an ocean liner. It houses the **Maritime**

Museum. On the left you will pass bocce ball courts as you come to the

beginning of the municipal pier. Walk out on the pier for amazing City and

Bay views and then retrace your steps to the promenade, turning right

towards the bluff with the old barracks buildings. This leads to Fort Mason,

an early Army post used for supply ships with provisions for the Presidio,

as well as a major debarcation and embarcation site for soldiers being sent

overseas. Today, Fort Mason is part of the Golden Gate National Recreation

Area, and its former military housing and warehouses now house museums,

live theater and a farmer's market. You will have to walk down the long

staircase to explore this part of the fort. Wander through the park, on the bluff above, enjoy the spectacular views and, if interested, continue to the left and the main housing area of the fort. Retrace your steps back down McDowell from Fort Mason to Aquatic Park and explore the Hyde Street Pier. Like an open air museum, the Hyde Street Pier is home to many different sailing vessels, some of which are open to visit, and each with an informative history. There is the Balclutha, a three masted sailing

ship; the **Eureka**,

an early ferry boat;

the **C.A. Thayer**, an

early lumber ship;

and tugboats and

examples of ship cabins to peruse. The Hyde Street

Pier is a perfect location to get a good picture of

what waterfront life used to be like in San Francisco.

Walk one block up Hyde Street to

Ghirardelli Square. Former home

of the

famous

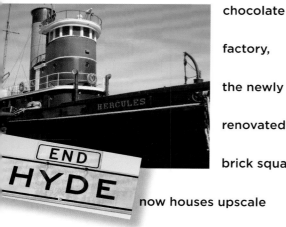

Ghirardelli Square

chocolate factory, the newly renovated brick square now houses upscale

restaurants and shops. Visit the

famous chocolate shop and café. Not only is

there chocolate in every form, there is also a very

informative exhibit of how chocolate is made.

Head back to Beach Street and continue to the

right. You will pass a red brick building, **The Cannery**, the former Del Monte

cannery now converted into shops and cafés. Exit

The Cannery on Jefferson Street and turn right.

Enjoy all of the many souvenir shops and galleries

as you walk along. You will be able to tell that you

are approaching **Fisherman's Wharf** by all of the

wonderful crab stands along the street. Famous

Wharf fish restaurants are on your left next to the

fishing boats. The seafood at any of these old,

established restaurants is outstanding. At Pier 45 is the **Musée Mécanique**

which houses the world's largest privately owned collection of antique

arcade machines and musical instruments that are mechanically operated.

Also at Pier 45 is the **USS Pampanito Submarine and Museum**, a fascinating

opportunity to go aboard a submarine. A few more steps down Jefferson

Street are the **Boudin Sourdough Bakery & Café** and the **Rainforest Café** —

a tropical restaurant which also teaches about the environment.

Cross Beach Street to **Pier 39**. This tourist destination has many shops,

restaurants, a theater, a carrousel, outside entertainment, and sea

lions living at the end of the pier to the left. You will hear them before you see them! Walk around the promenade to the right and to the far side of Pier 39 and you will come to the **Aquarium of the Bay**, well worth a visit. Just beyond is **AC SailingSF**, a new waterfront attraction where you can reserve a ride on USA76, an America's Cup racing yacht. The *PowerHike* continues to the left along **The Embarcadero**. You will pass many interesting

restaurants, the SS Jeremiah O'Brien at Pier 23, the only ship left from the World War II invasion of Normandy; and Hornblower Cruises, a wonderful way to see the Bay at night. Ahead are Pier 27 and Pier 29 where preparation is going on for the America's Cup Waterfront Village as San Francisco hosts the Louis Vuitton Cup and the America's Cup Finals in 2013.

Cross The Embarcadero at the Chestnut–Sansome Street sign. Turn right on Sansome

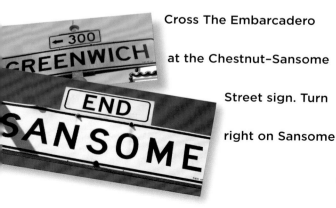

Street and walk to Greenwich Street.

Turn right on Greenwich to the Greenwich Stairs leading up the steep slope of **Telegraph Hill** (so named because of a telegraph pole to announce ships, placed on the hill in the 1800s). The steps end at the top at **Coit Tower**. Dedicated in 1933, Coit Tower was built to honor firefighters and

add beauty to the City and Telegraph Hill. Coit Tower

has an entrance fee to go to the top, and tickets are

available at the gift shop. You can enter just the ground

floor for free and view the 1930s-era murals depicting

scenes of California and San Francisco.

When you are ready to leave Coit Tower, walk around

to the back until you find the Filbert Street stairs.

These take you back down to The Embarcadero, and offer the most amazing vistas of the Bay, as well as the unique architecture and lifestyles of the residents of Telegraph Hill.

At the foot of the Filbert Street stairs is **Levi Strauss Plaza**. The red brick buildings house the corporate headquarters of the famous blue jean company, started during the Gold Rush in San Francisco. Visit the exhibit of the company's history, open Monday – Sunday 10 am to 5 pm. There are authentic old jeans which have been collected, as well as newer ones that were modified for rock stars such as Madonna. This *PowerHike* ends here, but enjoy one of the cafés along The Embarcadero or in the Ferry Building to sit and savor the delights of the day, or take a ride on one of the charming streetcars that run along The Embarcadero.

NOTE: On the way to Fisherman's Wharf on the Hyde Street Cable Car, get off a couple of blocks early at Lombard and Hyde Streets. Walk down the "Crookedest Street in the World"! Go back up to Hyde Street and catch the cable car down to the Wharf, or just walk down the hill.

CHAPTER 3

NORTH BEACH BARBARY COAST

DISTANCE 4 MILES | **TIME 4 HOURS**

WELLS FARGO HISTORY MUSEUM

TRANSAMERICA PYRAMID

JACKSON SQUARE HISTORIC DISTRICT

NORTH BEACH MUSEUM

JACK KEROUAC ALLEY

CITY LIGHTS BOOKSTORE

CLUB FUGAZI •
BEACH BLANKET BABYLON

WASHINGTON SQUARE

ST. PETER AND PAUL CATHEDRAL

NORTH BEACH

North Beach is the oldest Italian neighborhood in San Francisco, settled even before gold was discovered. Although immigrants from all over the world called it home, it eventually became a predominantly Italian-American community. The 1906 earthquake and fire destroyed the early settlement, but it was quickly rebuilt and the cafés and bars still retain much of their European

charm. In the 1950s North Beach became the hang out for the Beat generation and literary figures. The local coffee houses and drinking spots spawned the San Francisco Poetry Renaissance. In the 1960s it was famous for musicians and entertainers. The Kingston Trio and Phyllis Diller were discovered in North Beach, and Lenny Bruce, Jim Nabors, Woody Allen and local talent Robin Williams were featured in the nightclubs. Although Chinatown is infringing on the boundaries of its traditional streets, and some venerable old businesses and restaurants have faded away, the North Beach neighborhood still retains its original look, feel and flavor.

Consider this a gastronomic *PowerHike*. There are many restaurants, saloons, cafés, coffee houses, and delicatessens to explore. Each is worth a visit and it is impossible to decide. All are so full of personality that nothing should be missed. For location, ambiance, and a large menu, you could start with Calzone's. Try for a sidewalk table. We start at Café Zoetrope, in the famous flatiron

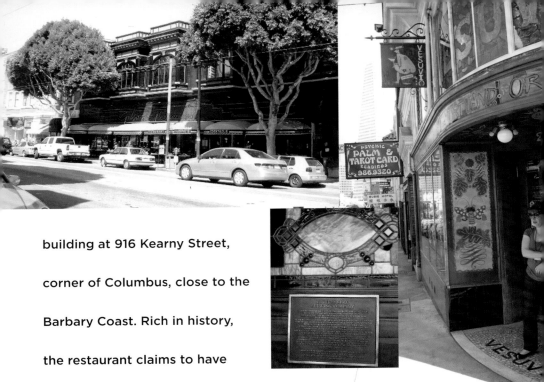

building at 916 Kearny Street, corner of Columbus, close to the Barbary Coast. Rich in history, the restaurant claims to have originated the Caesar Salad.

Walk north on Columbus Avenue towards Broadway, formerly the most direct route from the waterfront to downtown and the main artery of

North Beach, to the Vesuvio Café, on Jack Kerouac Alley, named after the famous Beat author. A coffee house and bar that served the Beat writers such as Kerouac and Ginsberg, it continues today to attract local bohemians and is filled with fascinating photographs. Walk up and back the short alley noticing the fascinating quotes embossed on the ground. Across the alley is the legendary City Lights Book Store, opened by poet Lawrence Ferlinghetti in 1953.

Continue on Columbus Avenue to Stockton Street. On the left, upstairs, in the US Bank office at 1435 Stockton Street, is the North Beach Museum. There is no charge, and it is open during bank hours. The museum is one room of old photographs and memorabilia of the history of North Beach, including the devastating 1906 earthquake.

Continue left up Columbus Avenue to Vallejo Street where you will see

Poetry is the shadow cast by our streetlight imaginations.

Lawrence Ferlinghetti

St. Francis of Assisi Church. Built in 1860, it is the second oldest church in the City. Across Columbus Avenue is **Molinari's Delicatessen**. Every inch of space if filled with all types of gourmet treats. It is a perfect spot to get treats for a picnic in Washington Square. At Green

Street go left for one block on

Beach Blanket Babylon Boulevard, home

of **Club Fugazi**, and the live San Francisco

show famous for enormous headpieces.

Beach Blanket Babylon is a must-see

and it is necessary to reserve tickets in

advance. Also located on the block are **Capps Corner**, an

old time family style Italian restaurant, and **O'Reilly's**

Irish Pub. Returning to Columbus walk towards Union Street

and Washington Square Park. On the corner of Union Street is **Mario's**

Bohemian Cigar Store. Filled with personality, Mario's claims to have one

of the best focaccia sandwiches in North Beach. In reaching Union Street

you have passed The Stinking Rose, where everything is cooked and

infused with garlic; Mona Lisa, Caffe Roma, Rose Pistola, Sodini's; and

the North Beach Restaurant, one of the oldest and most famous of North

Beach restaurants.

Washington Square is one

of the oldest parks in the

city, established in 1847.

Saints Peter and Paul Church

is on the north side of the

park, and remains an active

parish for the community. Walk around and through the park visiting the

famous fireman statue, commemorating the efforts of volunteer firemen, and the statue of Benjamin Franklin.

Mama's is on the northwest corner of the

park at Stockton Street and Filbert Street.

Continue on Stockton Street towards Union

Street, passing the North Beach Athletic Club. At the

corner of Stockton and Union is **Original Joe's**, a unique

SF experience. Turn left and walk up to Grant Avenue.

Between Filbert Street and Grant Avenue you will see the

giant gelato sundae at the **Gelato** café, serving the best gelato in North

Beach. Turn right on Grant to enjoy great shopping at many hip boutiques.

At the corner of Grant and Vallejo Street is **Caffe Trieste**, the most famous

coffee house in North Beach, where the walls are covered with old photos.

Every Saturday afternoon from 12-2 there is live music. Next door is the

Trieste Annex which sells coffee and coffee paraphernalia, and ships as

well! Turn left as you leave the café, and walk back over to Columbus

Avenue. To the left is **Biordi**, a store stuffed full of Italian pottery. The

display of ceramics is dazzling! Another tantalizing bakery as you wind

down this *PowerHike* is **Stella Pastry and Caffe**, a part of North Beach since

its beginning.

You have wandered the streets of North Beach, soaking up culture and history and watching the street life. Experience the vibrancy of life and pick a place to relax and enjoy dinner. Remember, each restaurant and café is memorable, so try to experience as many as you can in this wonderful *PowerHike* and epicurean adventure.

THE BARBARY COAST

San Francisco, the sophisticated City you see today, was not always so. The former Yerba Buena, as it was known when the Spanish settled here, went through a half-century of rough and tumble lawlessness. This did not stop

anyone from wanting to come here, and, after the discovery of gold, the City grew from a military outpost to over 300,000 inhabitants. Word spread about the wild Barbary Coast frontier town, where millions of dollars were made in the gold mines, and speculators rushed to make their own millions. Remarkably, remnants of this colorful

past still remain to be seen in their original location next to the Bay, in what is known as the **Jackson Square Historic District**. Located so close to the waterfront, this area was premier real estate and architecturally beautiful brick buildings were built here. Saved from the 1906 fire by a fire hose that came over Telegraph Hill, the buildings remained intact. It went through a period of decline following the fire, but as the City grew towards Market Street, the mid-20th century saw it develop into the vibrant area that you see now.

We begin this *PowerHike* where it all began – with gold. The Wells Fargo History Museum is located at 420 Montgomery Street, on the ground floor of the Wells Fargo Bank building. Here you can see real gold, a vintage stagecoach, and some of the equipment used to weigh the gold when it came in from the mines to be sold.

After your visit, leave the museum and head right on Montgomery Street to the corner of Montgomery and Clay Street. The Transamerica Pyramid building is the tallest in San Francisco – 48 stories, 853 feet tall. Turn right on Clay and walk to the eastern side of the Pyramid, and notice the small

redwood park, a green refuge within the urban landscape of concrete

and brick. Continue one block to the corner of Sansome Street and Clay

Street, and stop at the building on the northwest corner, where you will

find a plaque commemorating one of the hundreds of ships abandoned in the Bay during the Gold Rush, the Niantic. During the time the City

was attracting thousands to make their fortunes in gold, sailors on the

supply ships at anchor in the Bay would literally jump ship and head for

the hills, abandoning the ships to rot at anchor. These ships eventually

were salvaged to become places of business:

hotels, saloons, and stores. The Niantic was the

foundation of a hotel on this very spot. In fact,

the skeletons of ships are under much of this section of the City, as the

waterline of the Bay was originally very close to Montgomery Street, and

the shore was filled in to make room for commercial development.

Turn left onto Sansome Street and walk north three blocks to Pacific

Street. Notice the bronze Barbary Coast directional plaques in the sidewalk

that guide you along the Barbary Coast Trail.

At Pacific Street, take a quick detour off

the trail and walk right for one block to the

corner of Pacific and Battery

Streets. The Old Ship Saloon,

once an infamous drinking

establishment reputed for

kidnapping or "shanghaiing"

sailors to work on the supply ships, still stands,

and is now a bustling pub and sports bar. Walk one more block to Front

Street and Walton Park, a beautiful spot nestled in this area of new

condominiums and high rise apartments.

Retrace your steps to Pacific and left back to Jackson and Sansome Streets, and continue west on Jackson Street to Montgomery Street. On the corner is an original Barbary Coast-era brick and granite building, once the Bank of Lucas, Turner & Co., whose first manager was William Tecumseh Sherman, later General Sherman of the Union Army. Now go in the opposite direction (south) on Montgomery Street for a quick look at some original buildings of the period. The Belli Building at 722 Montgomery Street was

originally a waterfront warehouse,

built on landfill. The three buildings

alongside are also of this era. Across

the street is the location of the first

Yom Kippur service for the Jewish community in the 1840s.

Return up Montgomery to Jackson Street,

location of a wooden foot bridge over the Bay

waters. To the left is a lively restaurant, **Kells Irish**

Restaurant & Bar. Turn right and walk along under the beautiful old trees. Notice that the architecture on this block differs from one side to the other. The buildings on the left (north) side reflect the more somber Edwardian style, while the slightly newer buildings incorporate Victorian flourishes. Now the shops in the **Jackson Square Historic District**

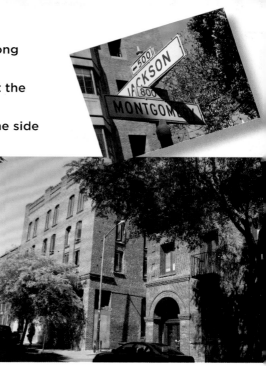

have become well-known for high-end antiques and interior design. Of particular note are the Hotaling buildings, at 445-473 Jackson Street. They are reputed to be the best example of 1860s Italianate commercial

architecture in San Francisco. Between the buildings is Hotaling Place, featuring period street lamps and even hitching posts, dating from the stables located there. The original shoreline of Yerba Buena Cove is represented there in the alley by the wavy lines in the pavement. In the middle of the alley on the right is the Villa Taverna, whose façade is built of cobblestones from nearby streets. Just left of the Hotaling Buildings on the right side

of the street is the **Ghiradelli Building**, built in 1853. It was the original plant of the Ghiradelli Chocolate Company. Across the street and next to the location of the former **Tremont Hotel**, is a little alley named **Balance Place**, location of the **Balance**, a ship docked at the Jackson Street Wharf and scuttled somewhere under this area.

Balance Place leads to **Gold Street**, where the first assaying office was located. The buildings retain the plain brick no-frills look of the time. When you reach Sansome Street again, turn left and walk one block to

Pacific Street. This was where bawdy entertainment reigned. It became locally known as "Terrific Street" because of all the dance halls, rowdy saloons, and brothels. It was a rough part of town, home to a criminal component, and particularly dangerous for those not spending their money fast enough. Following Prohibition it became known as the International Settlement. On the left side of the street at 535 is the **Little Fox Theatre Building**. Built just after the earthquake, it began as a shady

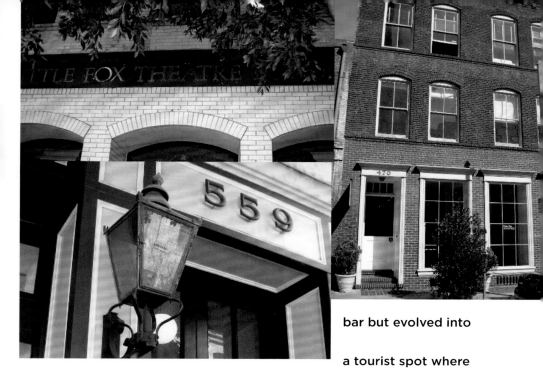

bar but evolved into

a tourist spot where

cancan dancers shocked the visitors and curious San Franciscans alike.

It was a distillery during Prohibition, and was eventually bought by the

Kingston Trio and turned into the Little Fox Theatre. More recently, Francis

Ford Coppola bought it for use as

a film studio where both *Apocalypse Now* and *Black Stallion* were made.

Another fascinating building is at 555 Pacific Street, the Hippodrome.

Originally named the Bella Union when it was built in 1907, you can still

see the bawdy representations of nymphs and nudes on the walls of the

exterior lobby. Across the street, at 574 Pacific, are two short, dumpy

establishments that were once dance-hall bars. One, Spider Kelly's, was a

particularly seedy dump. Shootings were frequent, and these dives represented the raw end of "Terrific Street."

Almost every building in this section of Pacific Street has a sordid history. Finally the community demanded that the district be cleaned up and policed, so the wild Barbary Coast was tamed. But the neighborhood still exists as it was, and it is a fascinating *PowerHike* through its unique past.

CHAPTER 4

CHINATOWN

| DISTANCE **2** MILES | TIME **2** HOURS |

San Francisco's Chinatown is a vibrant community. This *PowerHike* guides you through an historic neighborhood, passing through small alleys to experience authentic Chinese life and culture. There are shops and cafés intended for the tourist, but you will also experience the true nature of life in

the Chinese neighborhood. It is a dynamic and thriving section of the City.

We start at the colorful and welcoming Chinatown Gates on the corner of Bush Street and Grant Avenue. The gates are fairly recent, a gift from the Taiwan government in 1970. Note the dragon on top; it is a divine and mythical creature and a symbol of the Chinese people. The Chinese first came to San Francisco to work on building

the Transcontinental Railway during and

after the California Gold Rush of 1849. The

earthquake and fire of 1906 destroyed the

old buildings, which dated from the 1850s.

After the fire, the community was rebuilt in

the Edwardian

architecture common in those years, but with

the Chinese embellishments which were known

in Europe as "chinoiserie." Walk along Grant

Avenue looking up at the delightfully decorated

buildings.

Go one block on Grant Avenue and turn right on Pine Street to St. Mary's Square. Turn left into the square. It is a peaceful area in the middle of a very active neighborhood and there is a Bufano statue of Dr. Sun Yat-Sen inside the park. Walking left out of the park back to Grant Avenue,

you will see Old St. Mary's Cathedral on the corner of California Street.

Originally built in 1853, it was the tallest building in the City at the time.

Unfortunately, it did not survive the 1906 earthquake and fire and the

building you see today dates from after the earthquake. Back on Grant Avenue, stroll right and notice the dragon street lamps which date from the 1920s. This *PowerHike* is all about exotic sights, sounds, and smells. You will notice that most stores on Grant Avenue cater to tourists, with enticing Chinese art, jewelry, linens, tea pots, furniture, and silk. On the corner of Grant Avenue and Sacramento Street is the Gold Mountain Sagely Monastery, a fine example of Chinatown architecture. You will come to the Eastern Bakery on the right side of Grant

Avenue. It is the oldest Chinese bakery in the U.S., opened in 1924. Definitely try a moon cake.

Just beyond the bakery is **Commercial Street** off to the right. Stand at the corner of Grant and Commercial and look straight down to the Ferry Building framed by the narrow street. In the early days of San Francisco, business establishments lined Commercial Street, which actually was a pier going out into the bay. As the bay was filled in to make room for development, the street was actually built on top of the pier!

One block further down Grant Avenue, turn right on

Clay Street and midway down the block enter **Portsmouth Square**, an urban park, where you can see people practicing the graceful movements of Tai Chi and men huddled around chess boards. Return to Grant and Clay and continue a half block west to **Waverly Place,** a two-block alley full of various Chinese enterprises and, in the 19th century, home to many barber shops. On the top floor of one of the buildings is Tin How, Chinatown's most historic temple and the oldest Chinese temple in the country, worth taking the stairs to visit. Walk up Waverly to Washington, and across the street is Ross Alley, called

"the street of gamblers" in the late 1800's. As you walk Ross Alley, you will

notice signs indicating Benevolent Associations. These are old clubs which

date back to the earliest times in Chinatown when the Chinese formed

clubs for protection from resentment, discrimination and violence. The

organizations gradually evolved into more broad-based community groups.

Now they are primarily social clubs and meeting places for *mahjong*. Your

nose will lead you to the Golden Gate Fortune Cookie Factory. Go inside to

see how the famous cookies are made. The factory will customize fortunes

for you. As you emerge from Ross Alley onto Jackson Street, you will see

St. Louis Alley to your right and Duncombe Alley across the street. Former

homes to opium dens, they now resound with the sound of *mahjong* tiles.

In the next block are Beckett, Wentworth, and Cooper Alleys. From these alleys you get a good perspective of the past

and current crowded conditions of Chinatown.

Wentworth Alley was once called Harmony Street

because it was so beautifully decorated with hanging

lanterns and was the location of many fish markets.

These alleys today front apartment buildings for local

residents.

Retrace your steps on Jackson Street to Spofford

Alley, rumored to have been the home of Dr. Sun

Yat-Sen while he was in San Francisco. Continue to

Stockton Street and turn right, walking up to Pacific Street. This is the main

marketing street for Chinatown and you will find stores with live turtles,

ducks hanging

in the windows,

fresh and live fish of all kinds, and

not so long ago, live chickens. There are colorful

stalls of fresh fruits and vegetables, herbal shops

and tea stores, and throngs of Chinese. The street

is very crowded, but venture into the stores to

see what is there.

At Clay Street turn left

and retrace your steps back to Grant Avenue, turn

right and walk back toward the Chinatown Gates, on

the other side of the street. You will be surprised to see many things you

missed while walking in the other direction. Visit the tea shops and tasting bars and peruse the herb shops. Wander in and out of the tourist shops, always in search of the special treasure.

For the best part of the *PowerHike* enjoy a Chinese meal!

CHAPTER 5

SOUTH OF MARKET (SoMa)

DISTANCE 6 MILES | **TIME** 4-5 HOURS

FERRY BUILDING

THE EMBARCADERO

SOUTH BEACH HARBOR

AT&T PARK

THIRD STREET BRIDGE

CHINA BASIN PARK AND MCCOVEY COVE

SOUTH PARK

BAYSIDE VILLAGE

RINCON HILL

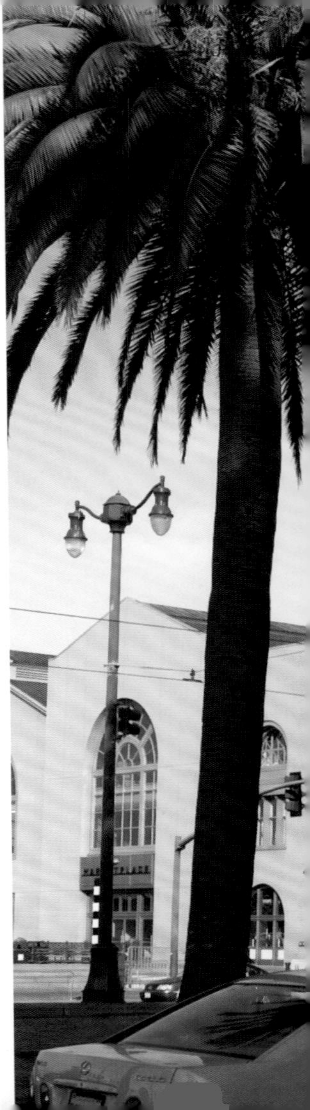

Palm tree-lined Market Street has been a grand San Francisco boulevard

since before the 1906 earthquake. Horse-drawn streetcars, horse and

buggies, motorized streetcars, motor

cars, and people on foot made their way

up and down the thoroughfare that runs

across town, east to west. The area to

the south or bayside of Market Street

is referred to as SoMa, an acronym for

South of Market. Once part of San Francisco Bay itself before it was filled

in to make way for development, SoMa has become one of the hottest,

hippest parts of town. A major reason for all of the building — office

buildings, condos, restaurants, and shops – was the construction of AT&T

Park, home of the San Francisco

Giants and one of today's

destinations.

We begin our *PowerHike* in front

of the San Francisco Ferry Building

at the foot of Market Street and

The Embarcadero. It was dedicated in 1898 and was the major hub for San

Francisco transportation for decades. After 2000, it was remodeled and

the interior filled with

shops and restaurants,

with an attractive

plaza and promenade

outside. We will save its exploration until the end of our *PowerHike*. Facing Market Street, head left on The Embarcadero along the Bay and enjoy the visual splendor of the Bay and the urban art along the way.

On both sides of The Embarcadero are numerous cafés and restaurants: **One Market**, **Boulevard**, **Chaya**, **Perry's**, and **Palomino**. Some are landmarks for many years, such as **Red's Java House**, steeped in the rich fishing history of the area. There are also shops for the rental of canoes and kayaks. You

will pass under the Bay Bridge. Before it was built,

ferries plied the water back and forth. The island

that you see under the Bay Bridge is Yerba Buena

Island, and next to it is man-made Treasure Island.

As you approach **AT&T Park**, you pass the **South**

Bay Yacht Club and **South Beach Marina**. It is one of

many examples

of the importance

of the Bay for

recreation. Java House, another quaint spot on

the water, sits at the entrance to the marina.

Follow King Street to the right and to AT&T Park. Restaurants around

the ball park are the places to be on game days. Second Street will be

overflowing with fans. There are also fan favorites on Townsend Street.

Enjoy the visit to AT&T Park and strolling Willie Mays Plaza. It opened in

2000 and has become a landmark in the City. Views of the Bay from inside the stadium are incredible and it

is one of a few ballparks where home run balls can be hit into the water.

Tours of AT&T Park are available at 10:30 am and 12:30 pm on non-game and non-event days and should be reserved in advance.

At the corner of Third Street turn left and walk down Third Street to the Giants Dugout store. Continue on and cross the Third Street Bridge, a famous SoMa landmark. Also known as the Lefty O'Doul Bridge, it is still

a functioning bridge and raises to let sailboats pass. As you

cross over the bridge, you will see McCovey Cove on the left,

site of the "splash brigade"— kayaks waiting for home run balls hit

out of the park. Continue around to the left and along McCovey Cove to

China Basin Park with the statue of Hall of Fame Giant, Willie McCovey, and

the giant concrete baseballs. Notice the Barry Bonds Junior Giants Field,

which sees lots of activity on game days. Turn around and marvel at the

view of the park and the Bay behind it. The baseball glove and Coca Cola bottle have become a recognizable part of the San Francisco skyline.

Retrace your steps back to the bridge. To the left is the University of California San Francisco at Mission Bay, and the surrounding biotech development. Turn right and go back to King Street and turn right to Second Street. At anytime, enjoy one of the many restaurants or continue

left on Second Street to South Park, an

oasis of green and calm in the midst of the

busy City. Turn left into South Park and

walk around the circle noticing the period

architecture, shops, cafés, and condos.

Relax in the park or enjoy one of the many

cafés. Return to Second Street and turn

right to Townsend Street. At Townsend

walk left and you will come to the South

Beach Village and South Beach Café. Go

left on The Embarcadero to the Town's

End Restaurant Bakery and cut in left to

the Bayside Village and the **South End Historic District**. You will be on Delancey Street. Above Rincon Hill, now home to a freeway, was the site of San Francisco's historic turn-of-the-century mansions. Look for the Historic Landmark sign featuring period photographs of the location. At Brannan Street turn right. There are new developments, and it is quite a hip part of town. Wander past the fun shops 'til you reach The Embarcadero and the **Delancey Street Café**. Continue walking left up The Embarcadero in the direction of the Ferry Building. You will pass the **Epic Roasthouse**, **Water Bar** (just under the Bay Bridge), and **Hi-Dive** on your way back. These are all noteworthy restaurants, and the outdoor **Americano Bar** at the Hotel Vitale is the

place to be for young San Franciscans on Friday nights. The Ferry Building itself is home to several restaurants. **The Slanted Door** is one of the most sought-after reservations in town. There are a number of shops for souvenirs, as well as gourmet food. Most of these shops have food to go. Be sure to visit **Book Passage** for some great reading. Allow time to wander through the Ferry Building, taking in the striking glass roof. Then, take a few minutes to reflect on your *PowerHike* and enjoy sitting outside, gazing at the never-ending activity on San Francisco Bay.

CHAPTER 6

LANDS END

DISTANCE 7 MILES | **TIME** 6 HOURS

THE LEGION OF HONOR

LANDS END COASTAL TRAIL

SUTRO BATHS

CLIFF HOUSE

SUTRO HEIGHTS PARK

OCEAN BEACH

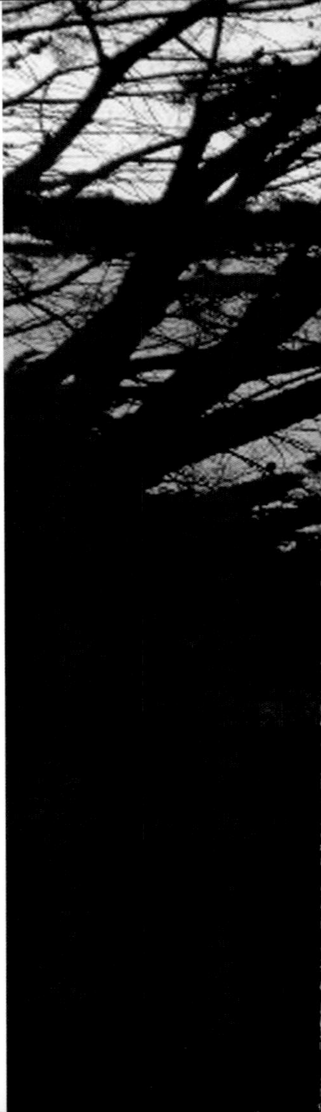

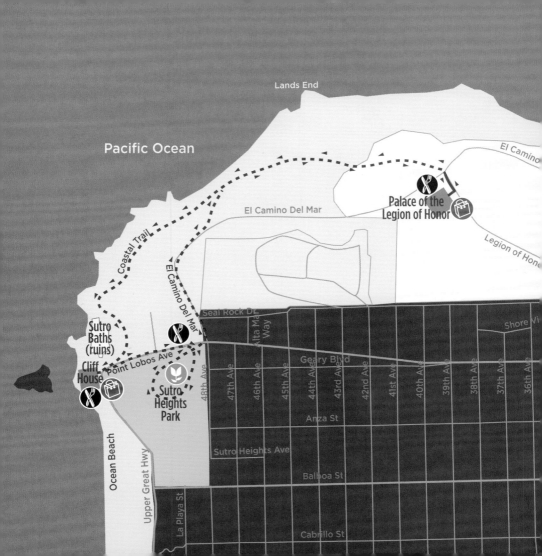

The City of San Francisco is on the tip of a peninsula, surrounded on three sides by water. To the east of the City is San Francisco Bay, to the north is the entrance to the Bay through the narrows called the

Golden Gate, and beyond, the Marin Headlands. To the west is the vast

Pacific Ocean. At the far northwest tip of the peninsula is Lands End, with precipitous cliffs and treacherous rocks where seals and shorebirds thrive, and the magnificent view takes in the fabled shores of the Marin

Headlands, rumored to be the landing place of

Sir Francis Drake in 1589. From Lands End on

a clear day, you can see the Farallon Islands,

27 miles out to sea, breeding ground for seals

and home to great white sharks. As wild and adventurous as it seems, you

can still walk along a very pleasant trail with wildflowers, stunning views of the Golden Gate, hidden beaches, and Monterey pine

and eucalyptus forests. You might even hear or see a

seal as the fresh ocean breezes make it a delightful

PowerHike.

The *PowerHike* begins at the California Palace of

the Legion of Honor, a Fine Arts museum, located

in Lincoln Park, next to one of San Francisco's most

beautiful public golf courses. The California Palace

of the Legion of Honor is a $3/4$ scale adaptation of

the Legion of Honor in Paris, and was commissioned by the wealthy San

Francisco Spreckels family to commemorate the California soldiers who

died in World War I. It is Beaux Arts architecture, with Auguste Rodin's sculpture, *The Thinker*, in the entrance courtyard. The interior of the

museum is beautiful as well, with a permanent collection of mostly French

paintings and decorative arts, and a significant

Rodin collection. There is an attractive café, and

irresistible bookstores as well. Just outside the

museum is the Holocaust Monument in honor of victims

of the Nazi Holocaust. Ponder the monument and the

beautiful City views, as well as the period lampposts, the

overlook has to offer.

Walk out to your left and

down the road bordering the

waterside sliver of Lincoln

Park Municipal Golf Course to the trailhead that indicates the beginning

of the Lands End Coastal Trail. You will find that the trail is very well

marked all along the way. The trail is only 1 1/2 miles, mostly level with a

few stairs. It is best to stay on the trail and not attempt to descend to the

beaches or venture further out to the edge to take photos. The ground

can be unstable and crumble, and the surf below is dangerous. There is a very strong tidal current out from the Golden Gate, and the water is quite cold. The views from the trail are stunning, and there are many opportunities along the way for unobstructed photos. The trail is wide because at the beginning of the 20th century it was a train track which took bathers down to the Sutro Baths, a significant part of San Francisco history. A staircase at Mile Rock leads down to a beautiful, secluded beach.

Mile Rock marks a buoy that warns

ships of dangerous rocks and, at times,

shipwrecks are visible.

As you approach Lands End, you can follow the trail to the right which

leads down to the remains of the once-famous Sutro Baths. The Sutro

Baths had both fresh and

salt water pools enclosed

by a soaring glass structure

— very popular with San

Franciscans in the early

1900s. The baths were

closed in the 1960s. Today, only the weathered and disintegrating ruins of the pools remain. The salt water pools were filled from the ocean tide which still laps over the site. You are now standing at Lands End, where the rocky shores were so dangerous that many ships entering the Bay foundered and sank. Rescue teams were called upon to try to save the passengers and crews, using ropes and pulleys to drag them to safety. At low tide you can still see the masts of some wrecks.

Just above the baths is the famous Cliff House, originally built in 1863.

There is an excellent restaurant, **Sutro's**, designed to resemble the Sutro Baths and featuring organic California cuisine. The **Bistro** offers both casual and formal dining, with views that take in the magnificent shoreline of Marin County to the north, the long white sandy Ocean Beach stretching four miles to the south, and the unending Pacific Ocean to the west. Reservations for Sutro's are necessary, but the bar area is available without reservation. *Hint: Sit in the bar and order from the appetizers — they are a*

great sampling of fresh, local San Francisco

cuisine! Take time to look at the historical

pictures on the walls so you can truly

appreciate the San Francisco of old, and

visit the gift shop. If you want to dip your

toes in the Pacific Ocean, walk downhill and step out onto Ocean Beach.

The water is icy cold, and there is a rip current that can catch the unwary.

Be watchful of children and those unused to surf. Remember to never turn

your back to the water. There are

"sneaker waves" that can catch the

unaware. On a clear day you can

see the hang gliders from the Fort

Funston bluffs, four miles down the beach.

Walk up Point Lobos Boulevard from the Cliff House

to Camino Del Mar. Cross the street and continue your

PowerHike into **Sutro Heights Park**. Enter the park

along the broad, tree-lined promenade between the

two lion sculptures which once guarded the entrance

to the estate of Adolph Sutro. Sutro was a rich mining

magnate in early San Francisco, who also served as the mayor of the City

and built the Sutro Baths and the original Cliff House.

The park, with its ruins and formal gardens, was his

creation and the location of his mansion. His home on

the property was destroyed, but the beautiful setting

and gardens remain. Check out the view of the City

from the overlook, and Golden Gate Park is just to the

South.

Cross back to Lands End Lookout, an intriguing shop

and info center and to the Lands End trailhead

and scenic view and enjoy the walk back toward

the Golden Gate Bridge. You will notice different

views and natural elements as you walk in the

reverse direction. Wildlife and wildflowers abound along the trail, but please do not disturb them. Be cautious of

poison oak as well. A beautiful red, shiny, three-pronged leaf, poison oak can cause an uncomfortable, itchy rash if touched. Follow the trail back to where you started. You can use your admission ticket to go back into the museum bookstore for unique gifts or mementos. Today you have

immersed yourself in San Francisco culture, nature, history, food and beauty — a perfect *PowerHike*!

CHAPTER 7

PACIFIC HEIGHTS

DISTANCE 7 MILES | **TIME 5 HOURS**

some short uphill and downhill

Pacific Heights is one of the most beautiful of San Francisco's neighborhoods. Since the 19th century, prominent San Francisco names such as Crocker, Haas, Lilienthal, Spreckels, and Flood built their distinctive mansions in this neighborhood.

Following the earthquake and fire of 1906 and the destruction of the mansions on Van Ness Avenue, Pacific Heights became home to the influential of San Francisco. The Haas-Lilienthal House, which still stands, is on Franklin Street between Washington Street and Jackson Street

and incorporates every possible detail of Victorian architecture. The neighborhood is not a 19th century

architectural museum,

either. Next to an Italianate

villa or a San Francisco Victorian you will see a 20th century concrete and

glass statement. The value is in the stupendous view — the Golden Gate

Bridge, the sparkling Bay dotted with sailboats, and the emerald green

shores of Marin County to the north. You will also see foreign embassies

and consulates with flags flying in the fresh ocean breeze. This *PowerHike*

winds through the elegant streets of Pacific Heights, to boutique-lined

Fillmore Street, down some marvelous stairs to the charming, hip Union Street, in the area known as Cow Hollow. Finally, it leads to Chestnut Street and the Marina neighborhood. Start at the corner of California and Franklin Streets. You can get here by cable car, bus, taxi, or car. If you choose to drive, there is a parking garage at 1700 California Street. Parking on the street requires a permit and there is a two hour limit. The large Victorian mansion on the corner built by Edward Coleman, forty-niner gold miner, is representative of the beginnings of San Francisco's fortune. Follow Franklin Street to the right to Clay Street. The white stately home on the corner belonged

to the Crocker family, one of the "Big Four" San Francisco names

(Crocker, Huntington, Stanford, and Hopkins) famous for building

the Transcontinental Railroad connecting San Francisco with

the eastern United States. A little further north at 2007 Franklin

stands the Haas-Lilienthal House, which was built in 1886 by the

Haas family, descendants of Levi Strauss and the blue jean empire.

Though only a block away from the 1906 fire, it was fortunately

spared and is an excellent example of Queen Anne style Victorian

architectural details. Admire the decorative features on the

outside, and visit the inside as well. Docent-led tours are on

Wednesday and Saturday noon–3 pm and Sunday 11 am–4 pm. The

tour takes about an hour.

Continue north on Franklin Street to Jackson Street and turn left onto one of the prettiest blocks in the neighborhood, location of the Matson house (founder of the Matson shipping line), now the Swedish Consulate. As you approach Octavia Street, the rear of the Spreckels mansion looms above you. Turn left again at Octavia Street, onto a short, brick street winding uphill. It leads to Lafayette Park, which faces the striking Spreckels mansion. The mansion was designed by the same architect who designed the California Palace of the Legion of Honor. This grand French-inspired residence was built in 1913. **Lafayette Park**, across the street, is a four-block

oasis with palm trees, Eucalyptus groves, tennis courts and a dog run.

Walk through the park, taking advantage of the

great views, and noticing the Queen Anne and

Victorian architectural gems that surround it.

Exit on the opposite side of the park through

the palm trees onto

Sacramento Street.

Continue to the right

on Sacramento Street.

Across the street is the wonderfully preserved

home, built in 1891, visited by the Sherlock

Holmes author, Sir Conan Doyle. Turn left at the corner of Fillmore Street to explore this shopping street. Follow Fillmore Street to Bush Street and then return on the other side of the street. Coffee houses are everywhere and you will find antiques, bakeries, flowers, clothing and jewelry boutiques. There is a neighborhood park worth a detour one block off of Fillmore Street, Alta Plaza Park. It is another lovely neighborhood oasis filled with beautiful flowers.

Return to Fillmore Street and turn left to Broadway. At the corner of Fillmore Street and Broadway, cross the street and notice  the steep stairs heading down to the street below. If you wish to shorten your *PowerHike*, take these stairs down to Union Street, and follow it back to Franklin, turning right to California Street. However, there is still much

of the Pacific Heights neighborhood to see, so turn right on Broadway and you will see an impressive white mansion. This was the James Leary Flood mansion, completed in 1913. Modeled after a 16th century Italian villa, it is considered one of the finest homes ever built in San Francisco. Turn back toward Fillmore Street and continue up the hill. Enjoy the beautiful homes with fabulous Bay views, many of which are historically famous. The gardens are beautiful, the doorways are particularly striking, and the various architectural

details are fascinating. Before you know it, you will be approaching the

Presidio. You arrive at Lyon Street and one of the loveliest stairways in the

City. Take in the views and beautiful flowers as you walk down the stairway

toward **Union Street**.

You are now in the

neighborhood known

as **Cow Hollow**. It

was once a lagoon

area surrounded by

dairy farms, hence

the name, and was the main road leading from

the City to the Presidio. Continue *PowerHiking*

to the right on Union Street, a lovely, old-

fashioned street filled with Victorian homes.

You will come to the Episcopal Church of St.

Mary the Virgin on the right at the corner of Steiner Street. The courtyard has an intriguing fountain, supposedly the last existing spring in Cow Hollow. As you approach the commercial part of the neighborhood, notice the shops are all in charming, preserved Victorian turn of the century mansions. Now they house trendy boutiques, galleries, antiques, cafés, and restaurants.

Meander back and forth across this relaxed street and the side streets as well. For refreshment, there is **Perry's**, an old-time favorite on Union Street, **La Boulange,** the very popular **Betelnut** for Asian fusion or the

neighborhood's famous **Balboa Café. Continue to the corner of Gough Street and Union Street to the blue Octagon House. There are few eight-sided houses remaining in San Francisco. Built in 1861, the designer, William C. McElroy, thought the eight sides let in more light for better health. There are tours on some Thursdays** and Sundays and the house is filled with American period furniture. Next door is Allyen Park, a small and very charming park. Back on Union Street, retrace your steps to Webster Street and turn right towards the Bay.

Continue down Webster towards the Bay, and cross busy Lombard Street. You are now in the Marina. One block

beyond Lombard Street is **Chestnut Street**, the most popular street in the Marina. Along Chestnut Street are popular shops, boutiques, national brand stores, restaurants and the independent bookstore, **Books Inc**. It is a hip, chic street, the place to see and be seen. The gem of the Marina neighborhood is the **Marina Green**, a large, public, green lawn stretching

along the Bay from Crissy Field to Fort Mason. This beloved space is well used by joggers, bicyclists, soccer teams, kite flyers, and people enjoying the Bay.

You have enjoyed the best of San Francisco on this *PowerHike*, and now it is time to relax and marvel at the rich life and history in the "City by the Bay."

CHAPTER 8

SFMOMA

DISTANCE 3 MILES	TIME 4.5 HOURS
FERRY BUILDING	THE CONTEMPORARY JEWISH MUSEUM
JUSTIN HERMAN PLAZA	SAN FRANCISCO CENTRE MALL
MARKET STREET	UNION SQUARE
YERBA BUENA GARDENS	MAIDEN LANE
THE METREON	CROCKER GALLERIA
ST. PATRICK'S CHURCH	MONTGOMERY STREET

We start this *PowerHike* in front of the Ferry Building

at the foot of Market Street. Market Street is the heart

of San Francisco and the main boulevard crossing

the City. Sand dunes until 1860, then horse drawn

streetcars gave way to electric streetcars. Some of the

 architecture dates back

to the early 1900s, while

new and modern structures tower over the old. Cross

through Justin Herman Plaza and *PowerHike* up Market Street, noticing

the contrasts between the old and the new. Streetcars and cable cars

still glide up and down Market and California Streets. On the left as you

head up Market Street are the renovated Federal Reserve Building, the

Pacific Gas and Electric building, and the Matson Building. Across Market Street are flatiron buildings which take up a whole corner and open onto two streets. The names of the buildings reflect the old San Francisco power guard, such as Hearst and Flood. At the corner of New Montgomery Street, turn left into The Palace Hotel.

Built in 1875, it was the tallest building in the City and the largest hotel in the country. It was entirely destroyed by the 1906 earthquake and fire.

The hotel you see now was rebuilt and maintains the grandness of the past. Walk in and imagine the history of the lavish corridors, and marvel at the elegant Garden Court with its glass dome ceiling and famous palm plants.

Turn to your right and walk along the wide corridor to Market Street, looking at the historical pictures on the walls.

When you exit onto Market Street, turn left and continue up Market to Third Street.

Turn left on Third Street, noticing the ornate façade of the Hearst Building on your left.

William Randolph Hearst was one of the

early powerful forces in San

Francisco. Cross Mission Street

and you are approaching the

San Francisco Museum of

Modern Art. With its

permanent collection

of modern and

contemporary art, it

also hosts visiting exhibitions,

has a fine photography collection

and the recently donated Fisher

Collection. The architecture and

the interior finishes and details are superb. Be sure to take the stairs for the remarkable views, both inside and outside of the museum. Walk up all the way to the fourth floor to cross the surprising bridge. Be sure to stop in the excellent bookstore before you leave. There is also a very popular café at the museum, with a wonderful sidewalk terrace where you can view the fountain at the Yerba Buena Gardens.

Cross Third Street from SFMOMA to Yerba Buena Gardens. The gardens are a venue for Yerba Buena Center for the Arts, as well as a beautifully landscaped park to relax and enjoy

the stunning vistas

of San Francisco.

There are good

cafés where you

can dine inside

or out. Explore

the complex to

find fountains,

flowers, and Zeum,

a community

art and technology museum, historic Charles

Looff Carousel, an ice skating rink and shop, and

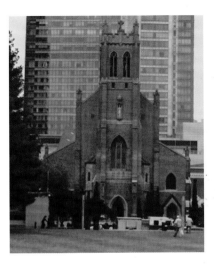

bowling center. The Metreon entertainment center houses an IMAX theater, restaurants and shops. Exit the Yerba Buena Gardens complex onto Mission and Fourth Street. Walk to the right on Mission Street to St. Patrick's Catholic Church, one of the few old buildings still standing in this neighborhood. Peek inside for a glimpse of the stained glass windows. Visit the dramatic Contemporary Jewish Museum. Further down Mission Street is the Museum of the African Diaspora. Yerba Buena Lane, alongside the Contemporary Jewish Museum, is home to a tempting

pastry shop, a Swiss candy store, chic wine bar **Press Club,** restaurants and the **Museum of Craft and Folk Art**. Return to Market Street and turn left to the **Westfield San Francisco Centre**. This shopping mall is filled with upscale shops, anchored by Nordstrom and Bloomingdale's. On the top floor is a variety of restaurants and just below them, a large theater complex. The escalator up into the atrium is a visual treat. There is a very high quality food court on the lower level which includes a

market and florist. It is a perfect location to pick up a quick bite to sustain

your *PowerHike* through **Union Square** and the **Financial District**!

Back on Market Street, cross to the other side and

visit the **San Francisco Visitor Information Center**

in Halliday Plaza. You are on the famous

corner of Powell and Market Street. You

will see street entertainers, and the cable

car turnaround for the Powell Street Cable

Car climbing up to Nob Hill and down to

Fisherman's Wharf. A cable car ride is a must while in San Francisco, but

save it for later, and keep walking up Powell Street to **Union Square**. This

landmark is the traditional center of the City for shopping, theater, and restaurants.

To the east of Union Square

is a famous alleyway, Maiden

Lane. In the late 1800s, the days of the

Barbary Coast, there were shanty houses for

prostitutes. After the 1906 earthquake and fire

leveled the structures, the alley was rebuilt,

and now, open only to foot traffic, it is the

location of upscale boutiques, galleries and a

wonderful café, Mocca. Enjoy Maiden Lane to Grant Street and walk left to

Post Street, continuing the *PowerHike* to the right toward the Bay. There

are several well-known stores on Post Street

to enjoy, but for a truly San Francisco shopping experience, visit **Gumps**.

Walk down Post Street, crossing Kearny Street, and, on the left, enter the **Crocker Galleria**. A glass-

roofed, European style shopping experience, there are flower stalls, cafés, and specialty shops. It is a pleasant

way to work your way to Sutter Street, then turn right to Montgomery Street. You are now in the heart of the old Financial District. Old Montgomery

POST Street has a very storied past. Immediately after the 1906 earthquake, a modest banker by the name of A.P. Gianinni opened a storefront and began making loans to San Franciscans so they could rebuild their homes and businesses. From this humble beginning grew the Bank of America. You can see the Bank of

America building easily in the skyline because it is one of the tallest Financial District buildings and the only one of dark carnelian marble. In the plaza in front of the building on California Street and Montgomery is a giant slab of black granite, nicknamed "The Banker's Heart." As you walk left on Montgomery Street, notice the

alleyways. Today they appear unremarkable, but in the early days of San Francisco they were anything but! In early San Francisco, much of this area was waterfront and very different from today. This theme will continue in the *PowerHike* that visits the Jackson Square Historic District and North Beach.

CHAPTER 9

THE PRESIDIO

DISTANCE 3 MILES | **TIME 4.5 HOURS**

In 1776, Spanish *conquistadores* and missionaries made their way north from Mexico, establishing defensive forts. One such fort, a *presidio* or garrison, was built at the northern tip of land overlooking the entrance to San Francisco Bay. It was dedicated in 1776. Since it was the northernmost military outpost, and difficult to supply, there were only about 300 soldiers and their families stationed there. After the Mexican Revolution, in 1821, Mexico began to colonize the region, establishing

Commandante's Quarters

Oldest building in San Francisco. Erected in 1776 as part of the Presidio and used as Commandante's quarters and headquarters during Spanish and Mexican regimes in California. Under the American flag used as headquarters, and now as the officers' club. Enlarged at intervals and restored to original architecture in 1934.

missions and large landholdings called *ranchos.* In 1846, during the US war with Mexico, American troops occupied the presidio. In 1848, California

became part of the United States. Shortly thereafter, gold was discovered in the California foothills and San Francisco experienced such an explosion of growth that the US government took it over for military use and it became The Presidio.

The Presidio was active in the war with Spain, ongoing Indian Wars, the US Civil War, and the Philippine-American War. The Buffalo Soldiers were sent from the Presidio to the Philippines and were the first African American troops on regular duty at the Presidio. The Presidio also played a significant

role following the 1906 earthquake, providing tent

camps for those whose homes had been lost. From

then until the early 1960s, the Presidio was an

important army post. It was closed in the 1960s, and

finally became part of the Golden Gate National

Recreation Area in the 1990s. This is an incredibly

beautiful area of land perched over the Pacific

Ocean and San Francisco Bay, with 350 historic landmark buildings, dramatic eucalyptus groves, Monterey pine, and Monterey spruce forests, and recently home to a 21st century filmmaking enterprise, the **Letterman Digital Arts Center**, headquarters for George Lucas' entertainment companies. This *PowerHike* is an adventure through California's military history, and a glimpse into one of its major industries today.

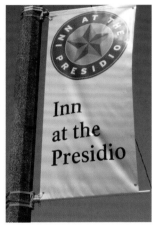

There are several different hikes through the Presidio. We have selected one that combines history with a nature walk and modern technology. Start at the Inn at The Presidio on Moraga Avenue. Built in

former Bachelor Officer Quarters, it is the first hotel

to open in The Presidio and maintains much of the

historical character and charm of the original buildings.

Leave the appealing porch complete with rocking

chairs and turn left, noticing the remarkable older tree

across the street. Walk past the Chapel of Our Lady

and the Officers' Club/Visitor Center/Archeology

Center to be completed in 2013, to Infantry Terrace.

Go right and you will see stairs on the other side of the

street leading to the Post Chapel. Go up the stairs, passing the Vietnam

War Memorial, to the chapel. Retrace your steps to Moraga Avenue to the

large square. This is **Pershing Square**. Named after General John Joseph Pershing, it is on the spot where his family died in a house fire. Notice the historic cannon. Adjacent to Pershing Square is the Parade Ground, now mainly used for parking. Continue to Funston Avenue and go left. In front of you is "Officers' Row," historic houses built in 1862, the oldest in the Presidio. They have been restored to their original beauty. Return up Funston passing the lovely outdoor patio of **The Inn at the Presidio** to the **Ecology Trail,** 1.4 miles which winds through densely growing eucalyptus trees,

ferns, and meadows, leading

you uphill to Inspiration

Point. Return to the Ecology

Trail and a little further

on the right will be a trail

that goes to the Arguello

Boulevard Gate and the

Presidio Golf Course, Clubhouse, and café.

Continue straight (instead of turning right)

to the West Pacific Avenue trail to the left.

Follow it, passing the tennis courts and

Julius Kahn Playground (El Polin Spring, a

picnic area is just down the hill) through the groves of trees. You will come to the Presidio Boulevard Gate, and to your left is a path known as Lovers' Lane. Used by off duty officers to leave the Presidio and visit the City of San Francisco, it is the oldest trail in the City, originally used by the Spanish to travel the three miles from the Presidio to Mission Dolores.

As you *PowerHike* down Lovers' Lane, notice the historic brick homes built in the 1930s for enlisted men. Lovers' Lane continues crossing MacArthur Avenue and a brick footbridge to Presidio Boulevard, where you turn

right and continue to Lincoln Blvd. One block further up, at the corner of Presidio and Funston, is the location of the original entrance to the Presidio during the Spanish era. Turn left on Lincoln to the site of the former **Letterman Hospital**, the first permanent army general hospital, built in 1899. If you continue walking up Lincoln Blvd., you will reach the former post office,

built in 1900. There is also a nice café and PresidioGo, the transit center. You can take PresidioGo to more far-reaching sites of interest in the Presidio. For the moment, however, *PowerHike*

back down Lincoln Blvd. veering

left to Torney Avenue and to to

O'Reilly Avenue, where there

are the former residences

of the senior physicians at Letterman Hospital. Walk to your right into

the campus of the **Letterman Digital Arts Center**. If you look inside the

entryway windows you can see famous characters

from the *Star Wars* films, such as Darth Vader. Walk

around the outside of the attractive buildings, and

notice that they were built with many environmental

considerations.

There is a lovely landscaped park surrounding

the campus, with a man made stream that meanders

down to the Gorgas Gate. Turn left and then left again

between the buildings to Letterman Drive by the main

Presidio entrance, the Lombard Street Gate, built in

1896. In a lovely patio setting you will find the statue

of Yoda, from the *Star Wars* films. Follow Letterman to

Presidio Boulevard to Lincoln Boulevard to Montgomery

Street and and The Walt Disney Family Museum, located in the barracks

built in the late 1890s to house enlisted men.

Through interactive audio and video exhibits

the museum traces the life of Walt Disney and

his amazing animation accomplishments. It is a

thoroughly enjoyable adventure for any age. There are classes, screenings,

performances, a café and store. The Museum is closed on Tuesdays.

This is a natural end to our *PowerHike*, but there is much left to see in the

Presidio. For those interested take PresidioGo to

the Log Cabin. On Storey Avenue, off Lincoln Blvd.,

is the Log Cabin, built in 1937. Follow Kobbe up to

Harrison Blvd. and Immigrant Point for fabulous

Golden Gate views. From Immigrant Point, you can

connect to the DeAnza Trail and Mountain Lake, passing the Central Magazine, and connecting to the right with the boardwalk to the Lobos Creek Dunes. This will add approximately 1 1/2 miles in each direction to your hike. If you have not already done so, be sure to get a Presidio map from the Visitor Center so that, if time permits, you can enjoy the many other trails of this beautiful San Francisco landmark.

CHAPTER 10

TIBURON BELVEDERE

| DISTANCE **5** MILES | TIME **5** HOURS |

BLUE AND GOLD FERRYBOAT
(PASSING ALCATRAZ AND ANGEL ISLAND)

DONAHUE RAILROAD MUSEUM

TOWN OF TIBURON

CORINTHIAN ISLAND

BELVEDERE ISLAND

CHINA CABIN

BLACKIE'S PASTURE

TIBURON HISTORICAL TRAIL

If you would enjoy spending the day *PowerHiking* in one of the charming

and picturesque outlying communities of San Francisco, the Town of

Tiburon — with its spectacular waterfront, wonderful restaurants, and

quaint shops—is a perfect choice, and it is only a short ferryboat ride

away. The ferryboat trip

to Tiburon is dazzling. You

enjoy the view of sailboats,

the Golden Gate Bridge,

the Bay Bridge, the East Bay hills, Alcatraz Island, Angel Island, and Marin

County in front of you, and the incredible San Francisco skyline behind

you – a perfect way to spend a half an hour. Purchase a round-trip ticket

at Pier 41 and board one of the Blue and Gold ferryboats to Tiburon. Be

sure to check the schedule for a return boat. In the late afternoon and early evenings on weekdays, the ferryboat returns to the Ferry Building, so be sure the return takes you to the right location.

Alcatraz, the famous prison, was initially a Civil War artillery post and is no longer a working prison. It is open to tours and a visit is a fascinating experience, not to mention a *PowerHike* in its own right. Reservations are necessary and tickets and boarding are at Pier 33 near Fisherman's Wharf.

Since the time of the Civil War, Angel Island has either been the site of

military protection of the entrance

to San Francisco Bay, a station for

immigrants coming from across the

Pacific Ocean, or a military fort and

staging area. Today, it is part of the

National Park System and open to daily

excursions. Boats can be boarded from

Pier 41, or the Angel Island Ferry Boat that departs year-round from a dock

in Tiburon adjacent to the Tiburon ferry dock. Angel Island is also a perfect

destination for a *PowerHike*. There is a five mile road around the island, plus side roads to restored barracks, and you can climb to the top of

Mt. Livermore for awesome views.

As you approach Tiburon from the water, the views are glorious. Houses

climb up the hills, boats sail

from the yacht harbors, and Mt.

Tamalpais looms against the blue

sky. Mt. Tamalpais is also part

of the National Park System and a must-see for another *PowerHike*. Upon

debarking from the ferry boat, turn right and stroll along Shoreline Park.

Not only are the views of San Francisco stunning, but also, this was once

the site of a railroad roundhouse and ferry boat loading pier. The Railroad

Museum housed in the Donahue Building is a few steps down the path and

worth a short visit. It has a working

model of the former train yards.

Continue on to **Elephant Rock**

Fishing Pier, a popular fishing spot

next to the **Caprice Restaurant**,

unique in

its setting

overlooking

Raccoon

Straights,

Angel Island, the Golden Gate Bridge, and

Belvedere Island. Return along Shoreline Park back

to Main Street and turn left at the sculpture, Coming About. Main Street, Tiburon, is one of the shortest main streets in the country. It is home to many enticing shops, and delightful cafés and restaurants, including Sam's Anchor Cafe, a landmark since the end of World War I. Most of the restaurants have decks

on the water with beautiful City views and make a delightful spot for refreshment. Continue to the right, past the parking lot to Historic Ark Row — more shops and cafés housed in arks that were once summer homes

on the water in this location.

Main Street, at one time, was connected to Beach Road by a wooden footbridge.

From here you have several choices:

1 Cross the street at the end of Ark Row, walk through the stone pillars at Bellevue Avenue, and walk up and around Corinthian Island. The views of the Bay and Belvedere Island are fabulous and, if you stay on Bellevue Avenue, you will end up back on Main Street. You will notice St. Hilary's Church on a Tiburon hill across the way. Small, white, and sitting by itself on the hillside, it is surrounded by wildflowers and is the setting for many local weddings.

2 Or, continue straight to Beach Road and walk left along the water for spectacular City views. You will pass **China Cabin**, the restored social cabin of the **Pacific Mail Steamship China**, open to the public on Saturday and Sunday afternoons during the daylight saving time part of the year. Continue

passing the San Francisco Yacht Club,

and follow the circle around and back

down Beach Road to Main Street. ③

Or, instead of circling back to Main

Street at the San Francisco Yacht Club,

continue on Beach Road around to the left and up the hill onto Belvedere

Island. The views are extraordinary. The streets are quite narrow so you

might see some

of the residents

riding around town

in their golf carts.

At the end of the

island, Beach Road becomes Belvedere Avenue, which you follow to Golden Gate Avenue. Go left down the hill on Golden Gate Avenue to San Rafael Avenue and turn right. All of the homes on the left side of San Rafael Avenue are on a man-made lagoon. You will pass the Belvedere City Hall and San Rafael Avenue will intersect with Beach Road. Turn right toward Main Street and you will have walked a big circle.

④ Or, continue straight to Beach Road and turn right, to Tiburon Boulevard. Proceed left, passing the Boardwalk Shopping Center, and continue on

Tiburon Boulevard to the

Tiburon Historical Trail.

The trail, "bike path,"

actually starts at the Donahue Building

and runs down Tiburon Boulevard,

ending at Blackie's Pasture. The trail is

located on what was once the railroad

track into town, and meanders along

the water's edge of Richardson Bay. Starting at the intersection of Tiburon

Boulevard and Mar West, the trail is 1 1/2 miles to the end and Blackie's

Pasture, home of Blackie, a beloved horse who lived in the pasture for

forty years. As you walk, enjoy the wonderful views of Mt. Tamalpais and

the hillsides. Return along the trail, which offers views of Sausalito, Richardson Bay, Belvedere, and the Golden Gate Bridge. Just before crossing San Rafael Avenue, on the other side of Tiburon Boulevard is the **Landmarks Art and Garden Society**, open to the public by appointment and worth a short visit. The Tiburon Historical Trail leads you back up Tiburon Boulevard to the ferry dock and the end of a

Powerhike that took you across the Bay to one of the Bay Area's unique communities.

Distance:	Shoreline Park and Main Street	2 miles
	Corinthian Island	1/2 mile
	Beach Road, China Cabin	1 mile
	Belvedere Island	3 miles
	Tiburon Blvd., bike path, to ferry	3 1/2 miles
Time:	approximately 5 hours	
Ferry:	1/2 hour each way	

CHAPTER 11

GOLDEN GATE PARK | EAST

DISTANCE 9 MILES | **TIME 7 HRS**

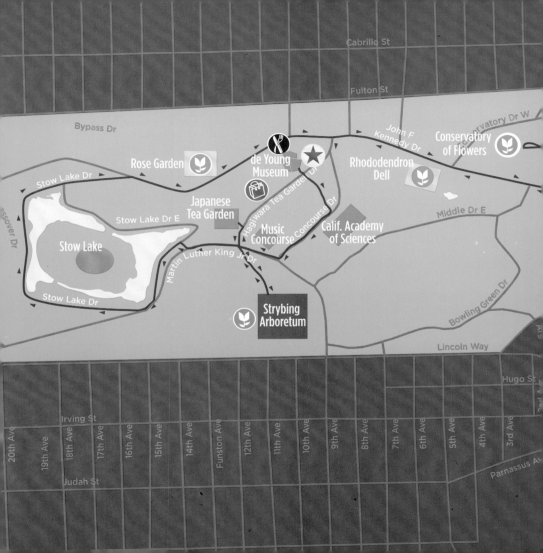

Golden Gate Park is 1017 acres of beautiful plants, trees, and outdoor activities. It is a glorious area of redwoods, eucalyptus, rhododendrons, grassy meadows and forested paths.

From windblown sand dunes, William Hammond Hall designed and created the park in 1870. In order to truly appreciate the hiking experience, the incredible collection of plants and trees, and the cultural features in the park such as the **de Young Museum**, the **California Academy**

of Sciences (which includes the Kimball Natural History Museum, Steinhart Aquarium, and Morrison Planetarium), the **Japanese Tea Garden**, the **San**

Francisco Botanical Garden at Strybing Arboretum, and the Conservatory

of Flowers, you could divide the park hike into two full days. However, if

you only have one day, or even one afternoon, choose a section of the park

you absolutely must see, and plan to return to the park at another time.

This *PowerHike* begins at the de Young Museum. Everything about this art museum is exciting and enriching. The architectural features are striking and the view from the tower is not to be missed. Definitely plan to spend time in the museum

and see the collections. Though an entire day could be spent wandering this fascinating structure, allowing a shorter time will permit you to see the other exciting aspects of the park. The café and restaurant are very attractive and feature fresh San Francisco cuisine as well as a spectacular sculpture garden. The bookstores are well-worth a look. Hours for the museum are 9:30 a.m. to 5:15 p.m., Tuesday through Sunday, and until 8:45 p.m. Friday evenings. Admission is $6-10, and free on the first Tuesday of the month. You can visit the courtyard, café, store, sculpture garden,

and tower for no fee. It is located on Hagiwara Tea Garden Drive.

After you leave the museum, walk around the gardens of the structure to discover sculptures and plaques commemorating events and prominent people from San Francisco's rich and colorful past. Immediately across the Music Concourse from the de Young Museum is the California Academy of Sciences. It combines the Morrison Planetarium, Steinhart Aquarium, and Kimball Natural History Museum in one sensational complex, with stunning

architecture and a 2.5 acre living roof. Walk across the **Music Concourse**

to the Academy, savoring the idea of listening to a concert from the

bandstand in this magnificent setting. A whole morning or afternoon

should be saved for visiting the Academy.

After circling the Music Concourse you will be at the famous **Japanese**

Tea Garden. Beautiful and serene, and still serving tea to thousands of

visitors, it does charge admission, and you can get glimpses of the interior as you continue on your *PowerHike* through the park. A short distance past the Music Concourse and bandstand and across Martin Luther King Jr. Drive is the San Francisco Botanical Garden at Strybing Arboretum. Enter through the Friend Gate into this vast garden (55 acres) of specimen trees,

lawns, water features, seasonal flowers. There is an intriguing walk through an international collection of trees and shrubs. At the far southeastern corner of the Arboretum is the Botanical Garden with the Fragrance Garden and Demonstration Garden, beautiful quiet places to enjoy.

The Helen Crocker Russell Library of Horticulture is here, with a good collection of botanical books and prints, and the Library Terrace Garden is a peaceful place to visit and relax before heading back to the other park destinations.

As you leave the Arboretum, continue your *PowerHike* to the left along Martin

Luther King Jr. Drive. There will be a sign for Stow Lake. Follow the path around the lake to the right. Notice the turtles sunning themselves on rocks. Ducks and other birds enjoy Stow Lake and you find people strolling around the lake or sitting on benches enjoying this scenic spot. As you continue circling the lake, you will soon arrive at the

Boathouse, where you can rent a small boat

for the lake, or even a bicycle to cruise

around the park. If you are short on time,

a bicycle would allow you to see the entire

park in one

fun day!

Retrace

your steps

back

towards

the de Young Museum along John F.

Kennedy Drive to the Rose Garden. You

find an amazing collection of all varieties of roses and a beautiful forest of trees across the way. Continue on John F. Kennedy Drive, passing behind the museum, to the McLaren Rhododendron Dell on the right. Spectacular in the spring, the dell is named after John McLaren, the Scottish garden designer who was instrumental in creating the park as we see it today. In front of the dell is his statue. Beyond and to the left on Conservatory Drive is the Conservatory of Flowers. The Conservatory is the largest glass and wood greenhouse in the Western Hemisphere, built in 1870. It is open Tuesday through Sunday, 10 a.m. to 4:30 p.m., and

admission is $1.50-7. After exiting the Conservatory of Flowers, be sure to

see the Dahlia Garden just in front, and continue back to John F. Kennedy

Drive, admiring the many statues along the way as you turn right and wander back to Hagiwara Tea Garden Drive and the start of this enchanting *PowerHike*.

CHAPTER 12

GOLDEN GATE PARK | WEST

DISTANCE 7 MILES | **TIME 4-5** HOURS

plus additional time walking the beach

THE DUTCH WINDMILL AND TULIP GARDENS

THE BISON PADDOCK

ANGLERS' LODGE AND CASTING POOLS

EQUESTRIAN CENTER AND POLICE STABLES

STADIUM AND POLO FIELD / LLOYD LAKE

DISC GOLF (FRISBEE) COURSE

SPRECKELS LAKE / MODEL YACHT CLUB

NORTH LAKE

BEACH CHALET / THE CLIFFHOUSE

OCEAN BEACH

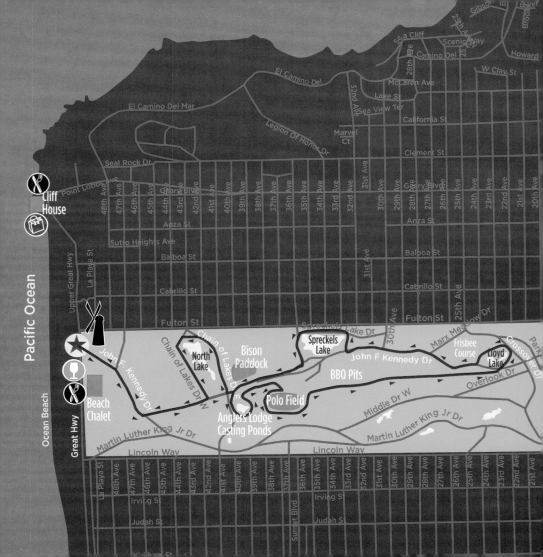

The second *PowerHike* of Golden Gate Park begins at the north Windmill

entrance on the Great Highway overlooking Ocean Beach. To the south is

the Beach Chalet on one side with wonderful views of

Ocean Beach, or the Park Chalet on

the other side, with beautiful park

views and dining on the Terrace or

lawn. This Spanish influenced building

was designed by Willis Polk and

opened in 1925 as a changing place

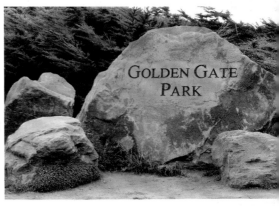

for ocean bathers. It was allowed to deteriorate,

but was reborn in 1997 as a fun restaurant. The

Golden Gate Park Visitors' Center as well as WPA

artist Lucien Labaudt's historic

frescoes are located downstairs.

Enter the west end of the Park

at the **Dutch Windmill** and the

Queen Wilhelmina Tulip Garden.

No longer a working windmill, it was completed in 1902 and repaired in

1980. The tulips bloom in February and March, but there are beautiful

plantings year-round. Follow the path along John F. Kennedy Drive passing

the archery field, the **Golden Gate Golf Club**, and take in the beauty of

the many varieties of trees. You will come to

the **Bison Paddock**, home to some of the few

remaining bison in existence in California. These

shaggy, peaceful beasts have been here since 1892, when the Park had an open zoo of wild elk, bears, goats, and other assorted animals. Cross JFK Drive to visit the **Anglers' Lodge** and fly casting ponds. The rustic lodge was built in the 1930s. The fly casting ponds are very popular with local anglers. There are even fly casting lessons offered here.

As you continue the *PowerHike*, pass the **Equestrian Center and Police Stables**. Just beyond is the **Golden Gate Park Stadium and Polo Field**. The

Polo Field hosts many different activities, from polo matches to soccer games, rugby games to cross country races, music festivals to dog field events. It is a lovely location to spend an afternoon. Beyond the Polo Field are two large meadows, Marx Meadow and Speedway Meadow. There are several barbeque pits and picnic tables. As you leave the meadows you see Crossover Drive and, beyond, Park Presidio Drive. It is possible to cross and continue the *PowerHike* in the east part of Golden Gate Park, or remain in the west part of the Park and continue around

Lloyd Lake and **Portals of the Past** on the left. On the other side of Lloyd Lake is one of the most unusual recreational

sites in the park, the **12-hole Disc Golf** (Frisbee) course. It meanders in and out of the eucalyptus groves and, with practically no equipment to buy or lug around, is a perfect urban activity in a stunning natural setting.

Spreckels Lake appears to the right. Circle it

and watch the many miniature boats sailing the

lake. There is even a Model Yacht Club. The last lake on the walk back towards the beach is North Lake, of the Chain of Lakes, home to unusual large cranes and other wildlife. Follow the path around the lake back to John F. Kennedy Drive and you return to the windmill and park entrance. Notice the incredible assortment of specimen trees and shrubs. Soak in the natural beauty of the plantings and the design of the gardens. You will also see statues dedicated to famous San Franciscans. These statues are not easy to find because the original landscape designer of Golden Gate

Park, Scotsman John McLaren,
hated statues, and even hid one
that was made in his honor! It
was later discovered and can
be found, if you are interested.

There is a map of the Park's monuments in the
Japanese Tea Garden or McLaren Lodge at the
eastern entrance to the Park.

Back at Ocean Beach, venture to the left and
the Beach Chalet Brewery and Restaurant
awaits you. One half mile up the hill to the right,
the Cliff House beckons. Originally built in 1863,

there are two restaurants, a gift shop, and spectacular views of the Pacific Ocean and the Sutro Baths. Retrace your steps to the bottom of the hill and, if time and energy permit, you can walk the beach (which stretches for four miles south to Fort Funston), watch the surfers, and enjoy the majesty of the ocean. Beware of the riptides, cold water, and rogue waves. There is a path that meanders along the tops of the dunes if you do not want to venture onto the sand.

As you walk, marvel at the fascinating environment you just experienced and the pounding surf at Ocean Beach.